The Wisdom of
Women's Golf

The Wisdom of Women's Golf

Common Sense and Uncommon Genius
From the Legendary Ladies of the Game

Compiled and Edited by Criswell Freeman

WALNUT GROVE PRESS
Nashville, TN 37205

ISBN 1-887655-82-4

The ideas expressed in this book are not, in all cases, exact quotations, as some have been edited for clarity and brevity. In all cases, the author has attempted to maintain the speaker's original intent. In some cases, material for this book was obtained from secondary sources, primarily print media. While every effort was made to ensure the accuracy of these sources, the accuracy cannot be guaranteed. For additions, deletions, corrections or clarifications in future editions of this text, please write WALNUT GROVE PRESS.

Cover photograph:Babe Didrikson Zaharias
Used with permission, courtesy of Fort Worth Star-Telegram
Photograph Collection, Special Collections Division,
The University of Texas at Arlington Libraries

Printed in the United States of America
Typesetting & Page Layout by Sue Gerdes
Editor for Walnut Grove Press: Alan Ross
2 3 4 5 6 7 8 9 10 •   99 00 01 02

ACKNOWLEDGMENTS
The author gratefully acknowledges the helpful support of Angela Freeman, Dick and Mary Freeman Mary Susan Freeman, and Jim Gallery.

For Pat Miller

Table of Contents

Introduction

For centuries, golf was a game reserved exclusively for men; women players were almost as rare as double-eagles. But gradually the doors of the golfing world opened to such stars as Alexa Stirling, Glenna Collett, Joyce Wethered, Babe Didrikson Zaharias, and Patty Berg. These players and their contemporaries left an enduring legacy.

The game's greatest legends — along with their modern-day counterparts — have much to say about golf and life. This book catalogues their wisdom. As you consider the quotations that follow, you'll discover that women players bring a unique perspective to the game. And you'll doubtless agree that their lessons apply to golfers of all ages *and* genders.

1

All-Purpose Advise

Amy Alcott once warned, "Never give advice unless you're asked." She was right. The links hold few hazards more perilous than a know-it-all golfer who constantly critiques her playing partners. But there comes a time in the life of every player when sensible advice *is* warranted. As Sandy Palmer observed, "We all need as much help as we can get if we're to play respectable golf." In this chapter, we consider an assortment of helpful hints that anyone would welcome with open arms — if she only thought to ask.

Play happy.

Domingo Lopez (Nancy's Father)

Good golf is easier to play — and far more pleasant — than bad golf.

Babe Didrikson Zaharias

There are no shortcuts to good golf.
The better players realize this.

Babe Didrikson Zaharias

There are no absolutes in golf.
Golf is such an individual game,
and no two people swing alike.

Kathy Whitworth

If it takes you a wood to reach the green
and your playing partner a five-iron, what's the
difference? Make your game your own game.

Nancy Lopez

If you have confidence in a particular club,
don't let anyone talk you out of using it.

Sandra Haynie

Golf is a difficult game,
but it's a little easier if you
follow your instincts.
It's too hard a game
to try and play like
someone else.

Nancy Lopez

Learning the fundamentals at the start
eliminates habitual errors later.
Babe Didrikson Zaharias

In golf, you may have to try a series of different
things before you hit on the best way.
Sandra Haynie

At the beginning, don't get fouled up
by trying to learn a million mechanical details
that feel unnatural to you.
Nancy Lopez

It's okay to struggle. The important thing
is to continue to try and work it out.
Catrin Nilsmark

I try to learn from everyone. I look at their
strengths and ask myself, "What can I do better?"
Annika Sorenstam

Always keep learning.
It keeps you young.

Patty Berg

Begin your play with a little warm-up session;
it's invaluable.

Sandra Haynie

The most overlooked routine in golf is stretching.
No one does enough of it.

Jan Stephenson

Before a round, don't hit a lot of practice balls;
just enough to loosen up and discover
how you're playing.

Sandra Haynie

Don't wear yourself out before you play a round.
Many a player has left their golf game
on the practice tee.

Babe Didrikson Zaharias

I learned early in my golf career to exploit the
competitive advantage advised by Walter Hagan:
Move very slowly before you play golf,
from the moment you arise in the morning.

Betty Hicks

Corrections that can be overdone are hazardous to your golf game's health.

Patty Sheehan

Women should experiment with their abilities. I don't see enough of that happening.

Sandra Haynie

I went at golf the way you learn to read and write: Master the alphabet first, then study and practice constantly.

Babe Didrikson Zaharias

When I do something, I want to do it 100 percent. I want to do it right.

Annika Sorenstam

M any beginners, and even some experienced players, defeat their efforts to play golf by depending on unsuitable equipment.

Babe Didrikson Zaharias

M ost women use irons that are too heavy or too stiff. The right club in your hand can make the game of golf much easier.

Sandy Palmer

S tudy the rules so that you won't beat yourself by not knowing something.

Babe Didrikson Zaharias

I f I were starting all over again, I'd lift weights and try to become tighter and stronger. It's a power game today.

Jan Stephenson

There are three things that everyone needs
in this game of golf — to keep working on your
game, to keep swinging so that you have the
same, repeating swing, and to determine
that you must make one less mistake
each time you play.

Patty Berg

When things aren't going well, I just try
to get out of my own way.

Patty Sheehan

Keep your sense of humor. There is enough
stress in the rest of your life to let bad shots
ruin a game you're suppose to enjoy.

Amy Alcott

Don't worry. Just leave everything
in the hands of God.

Babe Didrikson Zaharias

Golf, more than most games, has a number of clichés, often disguised as "tips." Watch out! Unless you understand these clichés, even a well-meaning partner can cause you to develop very bad swing habits with a generously offered tip.

Kathy Whitworth

Take most of the advice you get with a grain of salt. People mean well … but their help is not always correct.

Amy Alcott

The worst advice in golf is, "Keep your head down."

Patty Sheehan

2

Winning and Losing

Early in her career, Nancy Lopez received some simple advice from her sister, Delma, who said, "Aim at the hole and don't fall behind." Apparently, young Nancy listened carefully. She stayed ahead long enough to win a permanent place in the Hall of Fame.

A thin line separates winners from losers; nowhere is this division more evident than on the links, where an entire tournament often hinges upon a single stroke of the putter. The champion finds a way to make that crucial putt.

If *you're* searching for a secret formula to winning golf, take Delma's advice (after all, it worked for Nancy). Then, practice your putting until you can make those nerve-racking four-footers in your sleep. Next, memorize the quotations in this chapter and make them an integral part of your golf game. And finally, make a place in your home for all those trophies you are going to win.

I still believe winning is 90% mental.
You can swing a golf club as pretty as anyone,
but if you can't visualize making the shot and
believe you can make it, you can't win.

Nancy Lopez

The first time I won a tournament, the thing
that surprised me most was how many mistakes
you could make and still win.

Betsy King

I like the attention, the big crowds.
I like playing in situations where I have a
chance to win. That's what I live for.

Karrie Webb

Once I won my first Open,
nothing seemed impossible.

Annika Sorenstam

The difference between an ordinary player and a champion is in the way they think.

Patty Berg

When I played badly, Mom would give
me the shoulder to cry on, but Daddy
would tell me to pick myself up and dig in.
Pat Bradley

That's just a woman's personality —
a little more sincere, a little more caring.
Michelle McGann, on lack of rivalries in LPGA

I've won many times, but I've lost more than
I have ever won. Golfers have to be realistic
and know that they cannot always win.
Kathy Whitworth

My dad taught me I was going to lose a lot
more than I was going to win. So I don't put
pressure on my daughters. I teach them to do
their best — that's all they can do.
Nancy Lopez

Successful competitors want to win.
Head cases want to win at all costs.

Nancy Lopez

You don't see too many players win back-to-back tournaments. You have to let your mind rest and then try to get back in that so-called zone.
It's tough.

Tammie Green

When you are a champion, if you win —
c'est normal. Once you lose, everybody says you are over the hill.

Catherine Lacoste

The first thing I do after losing is to forget it.

Nancy Lopez

In golf, you must persist despite the frustration and the seeming lack of improvement.

Patty Sheehan

Golf is a game of misses, and the winners are those who have the best misses.

Kathy Whitworth

What does it take to be a champion?
Desire, dedication, determination, concentration
and the will to win.

Patty Berg

The mediocre golfer generally is one who
is too lazy to play better.

Babe Didrikson Zaharias

A young woman may have a putting touch
like spreading a hot southern biscuit with honey,
a tee shot that devours fairways, iron shots that
rattle flagsticks. And she may win, but she won't
continue winning, not without the B.D. —
the Burning Desire.

Betty Hicks

You try to go out there with the attitude that you're playing against the course. Usually it isn't head-to-head until the last nine. Up until then you're playing against 144 other players, and until the final round, you don't think about one particular person.

Michelle McGann

It's not good to want a tournament too much.

Tammie Green

Golf is only a game, and there's always another day coming up.

Nancy Lopez

You can't win them all —
but you can try.

Babe Didrikson Zaharias

3

Concentration

Patty Sheehan once warned, "On the golf course, you cannot permit mental wandering." But this advice was lost upon a youthful Nancy Lopez when a zipper broke during her very first professional tournament. Nancy admitted, "It was kind of hard to concentrate while wondering if my pants were going to fall down."

If *you* suffer from an occasional case of mental wandering, pay careful attention to the advice that follows ... unless, of course, *your pants actually do fall down.* In that case, it's time to call upon all your powers of concentration — and ask someone for a safety pin.

Concentration is the ability to think clearly
of several things in proper sequence.
Babe Didrikson Zaharias

The only part of my game that gives me
a big advantage over other players
is my concentration.
Patty Sheehan

As your golf improves, your concentration
will improve with it.
Babe Didrikson Zaharias

Brain power is more important to the game
than muscle power.
Sharron Moran

The single greatest lesson
to be learned from golf
is mental discipline.

Louise Suggs

If I could only bring myself to forget the excitement and importance of the match, I gave myself an infinitely better chance of reproducing my best form.

Joyce Wethered

Don't think about winning.
Don't think about losing.
Think about how best
to play the hole.

Kathy Whitworth

Your job is to get through the ball properly
by thinking properly.

Babe Didrikson Zaharias

When I'm on the golf course,
I'm at the office.

Patty Sheehan

If you have discipline, you can relax and
concentrate.

Sandra Haynie

Pressure makes me play better — it makes me
more aware.

Nancy Lopez

The mental part of competitive golf
is an overwhelmingly big part.

Nancy Lopez

Imagination is a tunnel and you've got all your
bad things around the outside. You've got your
view of where you want to hit the ball and you're
trying to hit the ball down this tunnel area.

JoAnn Washam

While playing, never think of beating someone.
Just think of the course.

Sandra Haynie

Golf is a spiritual game. It is like Zen.
You have to let your mind take over.

Amy Alcott

Golf is hard enough without having
ten different thoughts when you're trying
to make your swing.

Myra Van Hoose

There is such a thing as putting too much
pressure to win on yourself. Maybe you try
to force some things and that tightens your
muscles up. Who knows?

Tammie Green

Indecision builds nervous tension and
undermines any remaining confidence.

Sharron Moran

Between shots, I find it helpful to relax if you
just babble away about anything at all. It helps
you regroup and focus your concentration
when you need it for the next shot.

Nancy Lopez

Nervous tension is the biggest enemy in golf.

Sandra Haynie

Only long practice and the ability to think under pressure will enable you to hit the ball out of trouble under tough circumstances and prevent you from beating yourself.

Babe Didrikson Zaharias

I aim to have my swing so absolutely consistent that I never have to think about it. That's the only way I feel sure of what I'm doing, and being sure instills confidence.

Nancy Lopez

My work as an actress is on the mark when I'm not really thinking about it. It's the same as golf. You take lessons and you practice. Then, when you get out to play, you should just play the game. You shouldn't be thinking about any of that other stuff. That's where it's similar to acting. Erase everything you're thinking about: Just be clear and in the moment, and you can usually hit a pretty good shot.

Joanna Kerns

As long as I didn't think about it, I believe I could hit a golf ball well with my eyes shut.

Nancy Lopez

Whether you're practicing or playing,
think only of the shot you are about to make.
Babe Didrikson Zaharias

I try to treat every shot like it's
the most important one.
Meg Mallon

I try to put bad things that have happened
to me out of my mind right away. Over as long
a stretch as 54 or 72 holes of golf, similar
misfortunes are sure to overtake virtually
everyone else.
Nancy Lopez

I've learned to slap down any errant thoughts
that intrude on my mind. Kick 'em off the
premises and replace them with thoughts
only related to the shot at hand.
Patty Sheehan

Anger has no place on
the course. All it does
is hurt you.

Sally Little

I never want to think too much about how
I hit a golf ball when I'm actually hitting one,
because I'm afraid I won't hit it as well
as I seem to do instinctively.

Nancy Lopez

A friend of mine says good golfers play
with blinders on. That single-minded focus
is an advantage on the course.

Amy Alcott

To help your concentration, don't take
too much time.

Pam Barnett

4

The Women's Game

Herein, notable players examine the subtleties and pleasures of women's golf. If you're an aspiring golfer, turn the page and take a few lessons from the best.

Now we do not presume to dictate, but we must observe that the posture and gestures requisite for a full swing are not particularly graceful when the player is clad in female dress.

Horatio Hutchinson, 1897

Twenty-two percent
of all golfers
are women.

The Golf Channel, 1997

Almost any woman can play golf. It doesn't matter how young or old you are. Nor does it matter what size you are.

Kathy Whitworth

Golf is a woman's game. It does not require a tremendous amount of strength. It is not a contact sport. It is a sport in which women, by using a longer club, can drive the ball just as far as the men.

Kathy Whitworth

Since golf is a game in which accuracy
is more important than strength, a woman
can become a fine player.

Sharron Moran

Women are particularly good at those shots
which require finesse and grace.

Mary Mills

Golf is more than a passion. An obsession,
I think, is the word.

Cheryl Ladd

I think we need to get the message out to
women that it is OK to be an athlete.

Helen Alfredsson

I think it is both thrilling and wonderful to be
female, both in being a woman
and in being a woman golfer.

Nancy Lopez

One reason why golf is so
popular with women
is that it is one of the few
sports in which you can
compete and socialize
at the same time.

Jane Blalock

Golf is my job, but I don't know why you have to treat it like it's the most serious thing in the world. We're outside, playing a game we love. It should be fun.
Why wouldn't you smile?

Meg Mallon

I was born to play golf.

Karrie Webb

There is no better exercise in the world than walking, and that is at the heart of golf.
Every round you play means a walk of at least three to five miles.

Sandra Haynie

Golf is the best mild exercise for a woman.

Sharron Moran

No woman is too old to take up the game
and get genuine enjoyment out of it.

Sandra Haynie

I've come to the conclusion that this is a game
I'll never understand.

Helen Alfredsson

Golf is a game in which perfection
stays just out of reach.

Betsy Rawls

You never stop learning in this sport.
Once you think you've got one part of it licked,
another part goes — at least it does for me.

Dinah Shore

Women have certain psychological advantages in the game of golf. A man is expected to pick up a club and break 90 before he's spent 20 hours on the course. A woman is not expected to be so adept.

Kathy Whitworth

I once had an invitation to play on the Curtis Cup team but was five months pregnant and had to turn it down — it wasn't appropriate in those days to play pregnant. I would have played today. Things change.

Judy Eller Street

Don't be afraid to look unfeminine by taking a wholehcarted whack with the club. Anyone strong enough to lift a two-year-old child or tote a vacuum cleaner or a bag of groceries can hit a powerful shot.

Sharron Moran

Golf is golf.

Carol Mann

Women have proved they can do just about anything men can. They certainly can play golf as well as men, but they are doing it in their own way.

Kathy Whitworth

You know how women golfers are different from men? The men will tell you how good they hit the ball and how well they putt, and then don't.

Rhonda Reilly

Trousers may be worn
by women golfers on the
course, but must be
taken off on entering
the clubhouse.

English Golf Club Sign, 1907

5

Life

Actress Susan Anton, a 16-handicapper who once outdrove John Daly in a Pro-Am, observed, "There are just so many levels of golf. Every time you play, you learn a new life lesson. It teaches you patience and acceptance and so many other things. You never know what a day on the course is going to bring."

Thoughtful players everywhere agree with Anton's assessment: The game of golf has much to teach us about life. On the following pages, legends of the game share the lessons they've learned.

Golf is a lot like life. It will test your patience. It will dazzle and baffle you with highs and lows, successes and frustrations. Just when you think you've got it all figured out, the game jumps up and reminds you that nobody ever quite gets it.

Amy Alcott

Golf is just like life. You can go through a day of nothing but bogeys, but you might have one or two moments in the course of that day that are just so perfect that you feel like you can't wait to tee it up tomorrow and see what the day is going to bring.

Susan Anton

In golf, you win some and lose some.
In life, it can be the other way around —
you can lose some and then win some!

Nancy Lopez

Each time I tee the ball up I learn something about my swing and the game. That's what makes golf such a great sport: You always have things to learn, just like life.

Sandra Haynie

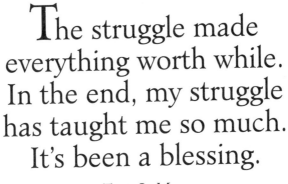

The struggle made everything worth while. In the end, my struggle has taught me so much. It's been a blessing.

Terry-Jo Myers

Rainbows always follow
rain delays.

Patty Sheehan

In your approach to golf, no one can tell you what to do. Just as in life, you are presented with options; it's up to you to decide which ones suit you best.

Sandra Haynie

The Swedish philosophy is that people are like plants. Some need space, some can grow close together. You need to find your own way.

Annika Sorenstam

We develop as human beings through the game of golf. We won't do anything that might lead to lower scores but might not be good for us in our lives as a whole. Who we are is, for us, always more important than what we do.

Pia Nilsson

I really believe that your entire lifestyle will be
a key to your tempo and rhythm. If you are
the type of person who hurries from one
appointment to another, if you do things quickly
and jerkily, that's probably the kind
of golf swing you will have.

Sandra Haynie

Before the final round, on a day of clouds
and humidity, Catherine Lacoste went to Mass,
praying no more fervently than usual,
for golf is not essential to life.

Peter Ryde

Every day I realize how fortunate I am
and how precious life is.

Patty Sheehan

Don't be in such a hurry.
That little white ball
isn't going to run away
from you.

Patty Berg

6

Attitude

Pessimists beware: The self-fulfilling prophecy lurks near every tee box, fairway and green. On the links, a negative attitude is the most dangerous hazard because it comes into play on every shot.

Perhaps no player, male or female, has ever enjoyed the self-assurance of Babe Didrikson Zaharias. She once addressed a crowd of reporters by saying, "Everybody come closer now. Today you're looking at the best." And Babe's words were not idle boasting; she backed them up on the golf course.

If your golfing psyche is in need of an attitude adjustment, the following quotations will help. As you learn to think positively about your game, you'll make the self-fulfilling prophecy your permanent playing partner. Together, the two of you will be a fabulous team.

The philosophy of "Think Positive"
    is an essential for winning golf.

Nancy Lopez

My positive thinking starts on the tee.

Sandra Haynie

My greatest strength in golf has been
my mind. I have always been able to substitute
a negative thought with a positive one.

Nancy Lopez

Think about where you *want* the ball to go,
    not where you're *afraid* it might go.

Sharron Moran

Imagine what you *want* to do, not what you don't want to do.

Sandra Haynie

My late father, a teaching pro back home in Australia, used to say, "Competence breeds confidence." He was right.

Jane Crafter

Coordination is almost everything, and the other big factor is confidence. If you have both, you've got it.

Nancy Lopez

I commit to a shot 100 percent and I don't worry about the result. What the ball does after it leaves the clubface is beyond my control, so I accept the outcome.

Annika Sorenstam

Give it your best, but always with the realization that your happiness and your livelihood are not riding on the next shot.

Jane Blalock

If you accept the philosophy that you will win some and will lose some, you've taken a long step toward "playing the game" of golf the right way.

Nancy Lopez

It's the way you feel, not the way you look.

Sandra Haynie

I know what it takes for me to play well. I don't get in anybody's way. I have to be happy with myself before anyone else.

Dottie Mochrie

She plays her best golf when she's loose and smiling and enjoying herself.

John Dormann, Meg Mallon's caddy

The more patience
you have, the better
you play.

Colleen Walker

Dare to play
your own game.

Annika Sorenstam

The best thing I have going for me, I believe,
is my attitude.

Patty Sheehan

I was determined to play the game well
or not at all.

Babe Didrikson Zaharias

Believe you can do anything,
and then take a stab at it.

Nancy Lopez

Don't allow yourself to be disheartened
by bad shots. Everybody makes them,
expert or amateur.

Sharron Moran

You'll see situations where somebody just
seems to play well at a given golf course or in a
tournament from one year to the next. My game
may fit the course, but it probably runs deeper
than that. It seems like if I'm in a good frame of
mind when I play, it translates
into playing well.

Meg Mallon

There are some difficult things about golf
for women to master, but really it's merely
mind over matter.

Sandra Haynie

Do your best, one shot at a time, and then move on. Remember that golf is just a game.

Nancy Lopez

7

Course Management

A. G. Mitchell, golf instructor to both Babe Didrikson Zaharias and Sandra Haynie, observed, "In golf, as in life, you can always know the direction you want to go, you can always know how you want to get there, and you can always think about it before you set out." Mitchell understood that the game of golf, like the game of life, is an exercise in forward thinking.

The art of course management is essential to winning golf. On the links, every player knows where she wants to go; a flagstick marks the spot. But only the best players know precisely how they plan to get there.

Women golfers have to play smarter because golf courses aren't really designed for us.

Beth Daniel

Course management?
It means you are in
control of the golf course,
rather than vice versa.

Patty Sheehan

A player must determine the best way she can play a golf hole, not the best way someone else might play it.

Kathy Whitworth

Play your own game.

Sandra Haynie

Playing strategy counts almost as much
as physical prowess.

Sharron Moran

I used to hit my driver off every tee,
then I saw some of the players hitting 3-woods
off the tees. "Ah hah," I thought.
"So *that's* course management!"

Patty Sheehan

Course management is the key to golf.
Somewhere along the way, you must figure out
how to get the ball into the hole
in the fewest shots possible.

Meg Mallon

Getting close to the flag is what the game
is all about.

Mary Mills

Never attempt to "press" a club by swinging too hard. Go to the next longer club instead of forcing the shot.

Kathy Whitworth

The five-wood is a great club to have. Many golfers have difficulty with the long irons. The five-wood solves most of their problems.

Kathy Whitworth

Playing with lofted woods is the better way for most women who play for fun. So add a seven-wood to your bag.

Judy Rankin

A wood is often the best club from the long grass because its clubhead slides through grass easier than an iron's.

Kathy Whitworth

Erase everything you're thinking about. Just be clear and in the moment, and you can usually hit a pretty good shot that way.

Joanna Kerns

Remember that it is the panic rather than the one miscreant shot which will make the difference between a good round and a bad one.

Laura Davies

In the rough, I think women are at
a disadvantage. Brute strength often is the sole
requirement for getting out of long grass,
and few women have that kind of strength.

Judy Rankin

Golf is a sport in which a woman has natural
advantages. One of these advantages is sensitivity:
a kind of perception that gets down into her
fingertips and comes out when she's holding a
putter. She "feels" her game more strongly
than a man.

Kathy Whitworth

Women can be at a disadvantage in the long
game, but in the short game, women are at
no disadvantage at all.

Kathy Whitworth

Arnold Palmer's mottoes were "Charge!" and "Go for Broke!" I not only think he had the right idea for winning but also the right idea for maximum fun.

Nancy Lopez

Every day you'll discover, when you tee up the ball, that you're hitting the clubs a little differently. You need to know that before going out on the course.

Sandra Haynie

Play the hole the way it was designed.
You don't want to leave yourself unmakeables.

Carl Laib, Patty Sheehan's caddy

Play away from trouble.

Babe Didrikson Zaharias

Consider each problem separately.
You're less likely to become rattled.

Mary Mills

So you play through it. That's what you do, you just play through it.

Heather Farr
On her battle with cancer

When I play my best golf, I feel as if I'm
in a fog, standing back watching the earth
in orbit with a golf club in my hands.

Mickey Wright

I like to look at the leader board;
I like to know where I stand. I think it helps.

Nancy Lopez

Spend a little more time in planning your shots,
and you will be surprised at the lower scores
that will result.

Sharron Moran

It's like you're in a chess game.
You're maneuvering for position.

Patty Sheehan

8

Mechanics

Here we consider the principles of a sound, repeatable golf swing. Sandra Haynie noted, "There are few perfect swings in golf, but there are hundreds or maybe thousands of good, effective swings. It's just a question of making the most of your ability and adjusting to your individual needs and your physical makeup."

For most of us, the perfect golf swing remains elusive. But an effective swing is not only achievable, it's probably good enough to win.

You need a proper understanding of the swing in its entirety before you can hope to play good golf.

Kathy Whitworth

You must keep the golf swing as simple
as you can. That is why I'm so adamant
about fundamentals.

Kathy Whitworth

I think golf instruction is likely to give you
more complicated words and actions to think
about than you can possibly swallow —
certainly more than you can digest all at the
same time while you're trying to hit a golf ball.

Nancy Lopez

Too many of us complicate our golf swings
with involved theories, when good golf
is actually based on a few solid principles.

Kathy Whitworth

Too often, golf instruction sounds like the
directions for building a lunar lander. If you try
to remember all the theories, your brain
will suffer a golf meltdown.

Nancy Lopez

The simpler I keep things,
the better I play.

Nancy Lopez

I just loosen my girdle and let 'er fly.

Babe Didrikson Zaharias

Before you can become
proficient off the tee,
you have a difficult task:
Remove any thought of
distance. Your main
objective off the tee
is control.

Kathy Whitworth

The most important thing
in golf is to return the
clubface to the ball
in a square position,
identical to the way
it was at address.

Judy Rankin

Don't hit the ball.
Swing at it. Develop
a nice, graceful swing.

Babe Didrikson Zaharias

Tempo is as natural to a person as rhythm. Once you discover your own tempo — and there is nothing mysterious about it — you'll play much better.

Judy Rankin

Thinking about smooth tempo helps me maintain consistency from day to day. The major benefit of good rhythm is that it makes it easier to control distance with each club.

Annika Sorenstam

Rhythm, pace, tempo. They're all connected to each other, and they're all a part of me.

Nancy Lopez

Each woman has to develop her own tempo. You have to find out what is too fast a swing and too slow a swing. And then you find what is just right for you.

Alison Sheard

You don't have to slug the ball
from here to eternity.

Sandra Haynie

I cannot tell you to swing slowly or to swing fast.
Every player has a different tempo.

Kathy Whitworth

Sit back and watch your everyday style,
and you'll be able to figure out your tempo.

Sandra Haynie

Finding your own groove is what golf
is all about.

Sandra Haynie

There are no absolutes in golf. Golf is such an
individual game, and no two people swing alike.

Kathy Whitworth

Your subconscious knows
what your special timing is.

Kathy Whitworth

It is in the hips and legs that women
have their greatest strength, and they must
develop this strength in the golf swing.
Sandy Palmer

The tempo experts tell us the backswing
is about one-third of the downswing speed, but
don't you *dare* think about that! Swing to waltz
music and forget about thinking.
Patty Sheehan

The rhythm of the swing will not change,
but the tempo might change as the clubs
change. After all, there are slow waltzes and
fast waltzes, but the basic rhythm is the same.
Sandra Haynie

The most important part of any good swing
is a good weight shift to your right side and
then back to your left side.
Judy Rankin

A good golf swing is like a baseball swing.
It's a rotating movement.
Marlene Floyd

Any woman who can dance can easily learn the footwork of a golf swing.

Marlene Floyd

For the average woman golfer, getting the ball
into the air is a problem. The reason women
have trouble is that they do not have much speed
through the ball.

Sandy Palmer

In any woman's game, she is going to need
a big turn and what looks like a lot of movement
in order to get clubhead speed.

Sandra Haynie

Too many women take the club back beautifully.
Then they tend to hit at the ball rather than
through it. So work on your follow-through.

Judy Rankin

Power is generated only by swinging
with authority.

Mary Mills

Dismiss the idea that a good swing is effortless.

Patty Sheehan

The only way for a woman to compensate
for her relative lack of physical strength is for
her to build an efficient, repeating swing,
with good balance and rhythm.

Mickey Wright

Women's great assets are their legs and hips.
They must use these parts of their bodies
for power.

Kathy Whitworth

Hitting the ball solidly is the key to winning
golf. And that's often what a woman *doesn't* do
when she has to hit a special shot.

Judy Rankin

Many times, there's nothing wrong
with your swing other than bad alignment.
Once your alignment is corrected, your swing
falls into the groove.

Kathy Whitworth

Right from the start, imprint on your mind
that you should let your clubhead do the work.

Marlene Floyd

The hands are your only contact with the club.
Make sure you have a proper grip.

Kathy Whitworth

A faulty grip leads to more trouble
than any other error you can commit.

Babe Didrikson Zaharias

Your hands are the only part of your body
that touches the club. If your hands are out of
position, your club will be out of position.

Sandra Haynie

Don't slug the ball. Acquire a swing that gives
you the feeling that your hands and shoulders
are doing the work.

Babe Didrikson Zaharias

The most important things are good stance
and good grip. Without these two parts of the
game, you're lost. After that comes good timing
and good balance. If you have these four parts
of your swing under control,
you'll do all right.

Sandra Haynie

The golfer's stance is a bit like a child's
play swing: something has to be stationary
for the swing to work.

Kathy Whitworth

The whole swing is really a piece of art.
It has its own dimensions, its own aesthetics.
A smooth, steady swing is a thing of beauty.

Judy Rankin

The swing will govern your golf game.
It must follow that it also will be a determining
factor in the pleasure you derive from golf.

Babe Didrikson Zaharias

I can't play by mechanics.
I play by feel.

Patty Sheehan

I don't think anyone
can help you with the feel
of your swing.

Karrie Webb

Someone told me long ago that the longer
the club travels toward the target, the longer
the ball will go straight. It's true.

Judy Rankin

When I start my swing, my paramount
thought is to not quit hitting the ball.

Babe Didrikson Zaharias

Keep a picture of the follow-through in your
head. If you get a clear picture in your mind of
what you want to do, and you understand it,
then your body will do it.

Marlene Floyd

As long as your swing works, use it.
When it stops working, change.

Lee Trevino to 12-year-old Nancy Lopez

9

Practice

Judy Rankin correctly observed, "All golfers, men and women, professional and amateur, are united by one thing: their desire to improve." Rankin might have added that improvement rarely occurs on the course; it usually happens on practice tees and greens.

If you'd like to improve your game, take a few lessons to solidify the fundamentals of your swing. Then spend a little less time playing and a little more time practicing. On the links, practice doesn't make perfect, but practice makes progress. And that's what makes golfing fun.

There is nothing in the game of golf
that can't be improved upon — if you practice.

Patty Berg

Take lessons, read good books on golf,
watch good players, and start out by practicing
with your medium irons.

Marlene Floyd

Learning comes through practice.

Sandra Haynie

Practice should be approached as just about
the most pleasant recreation ever devised,
besides being a necessary part of golf.

Babe Didrikson Zaharias

When I was younger I hit balls until my
hands bled, and I putted until my feet hurt
so badly I couldn't stand on them.

Nancy Lopez

If you can afford only one lesson, tell the pro
you want it on the fundamentals: the grip,
the stance, and the alignment.

Nancy Lopez

For women beginning golf, I stress the
fundamentals. It's a mistake simply to pick up a
club and start swinging. Take lessons
from a competent professional —
it's worth the money!

Kathy Whitworth

Correct instruction and long practice
win for me.

Babe Didrikson Zaharias

Your best preparation for anything is practice
and the formation of good habits.

Sandra Haynie

The more I improved,
the more I enjoyed practice.

Babe Didrikson Zaharias

Don't practice when you are too tired to concentrate. That will make practice a drudgery and will do more harm than good.

Babe Didrikson Zaharias

Never practice without a thought in mind.

Nancy Lopez

Practice as though you're playing your favorite golf holes. Don't just beat on golf balls.

Patty Sheehan

Practice with a purpose.

Babe Didrikson Zaharias

The basic parts of the swing must be understood
and practiced by any woman who expects
to play good golf.

Sandy Palmer

Don't be too anxious to see good results
on the scoreboard until you've fully absorbed the
principles of the golf swing on the practice tee.

Louise Suggs

Be patient. Acquiring finesse takes time.

Amy Alcott

When you practice, you know exactly what's
going to happen under pressure.
When you don't, you worry.

Nancy Lopez

A good golf swing is like a chain reaction,
　　　with one sequence of events
　　　easily following another.

Sandra Haynie

Find a swing that feels comfortable
　　　and works for you, and then practice
　　　until you can groove the swing.

Nancy Lopez

I don't count numbers or whistle a happy
　　　tune, but constant practice has established
　　　a rhythm so that I can now count on it.

Nancy Lopez

From the time I was 13 until the time I was 15,
　　　I hit so many golf balls I hated it.
　　　But now, I'm grateful I did.

Kelly Robbins

Repetition is the key
to good habits, in golf
and in life.

Sandra Haynie

One of the best exercises for golf is to take a bucket of range balls out to a challenging length of the uncut and hit them out.

Patty Sheehan

For me, the driving range is very liberating because of it's endless opportunities. You're not keeping score, so you can really live in a world of denial.

Susan Anton

Don't be in a hurry to get onto the golf course. The more time you spend on the practice tee or at a driving range, the better your actual style of play will be. Get your swing down before going out on the course.

Kathy Whitworth

I always finish off a practice session by going to the practice green.

Nancy Lopez

The more you practice,
the better. But in any case,
practice more than
you play.

Babe Didrikson Zaharias

You find talent,
not by looking for it,
but by working for it.

Nancy Lopez

10

Putting

An old adage advises golfers to "miss 'em quick." But Nancy Lopez espouses a different philosophy. She says, "*Make* 'em quick." The following quotations show us how.

Most fine putters are putters subconsciously. Putting is a psychology, not a system.

Mickey Wright

Putting is one place on the golf course where women are definitely equal to men.

Pam Barnett

Long drives are crowd pleasers,
   but a hot putter wins golf tournaments.

Michelle McGann

You can't compete if you can't putt.

Laura Davies

Anytime somebody is on a hot putting streak
   in a tournament, she's probably the winner.

Nancy Lopez

The putt is the payoff in golf. Unless you can putt well, the rest is merely exercise.

Sandra Haynie

No single set of rules applies to putting.
Whatever works best for you is the key
to putting.

Sandra Haynie

Routine is important in putting.

Judy Rankin

Putting skill develops from practice,
practice, practice.

Nancy Lopez

Putting is probably the most individual part
of the game.

Kathy Whitworth

Every putt looks difficult if it can win
for you.

Cindy Figg-Currier

After having a baby,
I have a new perspective.
Four-footers aren't
as important any more.

Colleen Walker

There's an old saying, "It's a poor craftsman who blames his tools." It's usually the player who misses those three-footers, not the putter.

Kathy Whitworth

After a great chip, the tendency is to let up. Don't! What's the use of chipping the ball to within four feet if you miss the putt?

Annika Sorenstam

Think about the last time you had a good round. I bet you made a lot of short putts.

Jane Crafter

Practice the really important putts: the five and six-footers.

Nancy Lopez

Most people three-putt not because they misread the break but because they didn't hit the putt with the correct speed.

Nancy Lopez

To be a reasonably good putter, you must believe you are going to make the putt every time. This is especially true of five and six-foot putts.

Pam Barnett

When you're standing over a short putt, focus on the ball, not the hole.

Judy Rankin

Always expect to make your short putts. Always.

Jane Crafter

The place where lack of confidence shows up
with catastrophic results is most often
on the greens.

Nancy Lopez

Don't second-guess yourself out of a putt.

Pam Barnett

Address the putt with your eyes directly
over the ball.

Kathy Whitworth

You rarely get the "yips" on long putts.
But on short putts you want to "peek"
at the hole. Darting, jumpy eyes
are a big cause of the "yips."

Judy Rankin

One of my bad habits is to follow the putt
with my eyes instead of keeping my head down
through the stroke. When I move my head,
I tend to come up and out of the putt,
pushing the ball to the right.

Beth Daniel

On short putts especially,
    move as few body parts as possible.

Jane Crafter

If your head moves, your blade moves,
    just enough to make you miss the putt.

Judy Rankin

Green-reading is an art, not a science.

Judy Rankin

Putting is feel!

Kathy Whitworth

Putt without agonizing over it.

Nancy Lopez

Practicing putting religiously is
   the most important thing in golf.
                                    Nancy Lopez

Concentrate on the things you need to do
   to make a putt, *not* on the consequences
              if you miss.
                                    Kathy Whitworth

Good short putting is about proper technique
              and the right mind-set.
                                    Jane Crafter

Putting: where the champions get their edge
              over the very good players.
                                    Nancy Lopez

The big secret to putting is to relax.
                                    Kathy Whitworth

11

Observations about Girls, Guys, Great Players and the Game of Golf

We conclude with a potpourri of wisdom about golf and the women who play it. Enjoy.

You're never too old to play golf. If you can walk, you can play.

Louise Suggs

When I'm off the course,
I know how old I am.
When I'm on the golf
course, I'm a kid again.

JoAnne Carner

With the guys, it seems like every shot has to be perfect looking, or they just give up.

Annika Sorenstam

Women who seek equality with men lack ambition.

Bumper sticker on Patty Sheehan's car

If you win through bad sportsmanship,
that's no real victory.

Babe Didrikson Zaharias

The game is the thing — not gamesmanship.

Nancy Lopez

There are times when a golfer is tempted
to throw her clubs away and forget the whole
"humblin' business." At other times, she
wouldn't trade places with a queen — that's
when the shots are long and true,
and putts are dropping.

Babe Didrikson Zaharias

I love to play golf. Even when I'm playing badly
I love it.

Nancy Lopez

When I'm playing, I'm having a good time.
When I'm playing well, I'm having a better time.

Patty Sheehan

Some of us are fortunate enough to play
championship golf, but this isn't essential
in the enjoyment of the game.

Babe Didrikson Zaharias

There is nothing like stepping onto a golf course
on a clear fresh morning.

Kathy Whitworth

It's the only game that you play
in God's arena.

Susan Anton

Golf gets under your skin.
It really becomes part of your life.

Cheryl Ladd

I played many sports, but when that golf bug
hit me, it was permanent.

Babe Didrikson Zaharias

No golfer has stood out so far ahead of his or her contemporaries as Lady Heathcoat-Amory, in the days when she was Joyce Wethered.

Henry Cotton

I have no hesitancy in saying that, accounting for the unavoidable handicap of a woman's lesser physical strength, Joyce Wethered is the finest golfer I have ever seen.

R. T. Jones, Jr.

Few men or women have come closer to mastering any game than Babe Didrikson Zaharias.

Walter Hagan

Ladies and gentlemen, I should like to pay tribute to Mrs. Zaharias, Babe Didrikson.

President Dwight D. Eisenhower, September 1956

Mickey Wright got the outside world to take a second hard look at women golfers, and when they looked, they discovered the rest of us.

Judy Rankin

The surprise has worn off for all of us because by now we are familiar with the brilliance of Catherine Lacoste's game. We accept that she can hit the ball harder and straighter than any living woman, that she has more confidence to play the 1-iron than do most men.

Peter Ryde, 1969

I remember playing my first practice round with JoAnne Carner and I could barely *breathe*. And I was a professional!

Meg Mallon

Nancy Lopez plays by feel. All her senses come into play. That's when golf is an art. She has a sense of self, and that's all you really need.

Carol Mann

Early in my amateur career, I was lucky enough to see Carol Mann and Kathy Whitworth play. I saw that each of them anchored her left foot on the ground and didn't allow the heel to come up, and it struck me as logical. It made my backswing tighter, and it's been a part of my technique ever since.

Nancy Lopez

To be the best, learn from the best.
Babe Didrikson Zaharias

This is a game that you never try to understand.
You just try to play it as well as you can.
Helen Alfredsson

No one ever conquers golf.
Kathy Whitworth

That little ball won't move until you hit it,
and there's nothing you can do for it
after it has gone.
Babe Didrikson Zaharias

Feel is what golf is all about.
Jackie Pung

My rhythm, my music, comes out on the
course, with the soft breezes blowing, the solid
click of the club against the ball, and then the
most satisfying of all final notes — when the ball
drops into the cup.
Sandra Haynie

Golf has been great for me and has provided me with a zillion delightful experiences.

Patty Berg

As women, we always feel guilty about not doing something for our kids — and then we end up not doing *anything* for ourselves. I've realized I can do both.

Nancy Lopez

Golf is a game of coordination, rhythm and grace; women have these to a high degree.

Babe Didrikson Zaharias

The shots around the green — the short game — can become the best part of any woman's game.

Amy Alcott

A slight variation on a theme can make the difference between a beautiful symphony and a collection of sour notes.

Sandra Haynie

I sang *The Star Spangled Banner* at the
Super Bowl and it is not as difficult as trying to
swing a golf club when there's a camera on you.
Cheryl Ladd

I think some of the golfers should loosen up
a bit and talk to the galleries. It's a sport,
but it is also entertainment.
Anne Murray

The biggest weakness in my game is that
I have fun with the galleries. I just love a gallery.
Babe Didrikson Zaharias

Part of my philosophy is that a gallery,
far from upsetting me, psyches me up.
Nancy Lopez

Make sure that the career you choose is one you enjoy. If you don't enjoy what you are doing, it will be difficult to give the extra time, effort and devotion it takes to be a success.

Kathy Whitworth

Golf and fashion go hand-in-hand.

Michelle McGann

I don't try to be in the spotlight. I like my game to speak for itself.

Annika Sorenstam

It's just a question of ego: whether a man will admit that he learned something by watching a woman.

Sandra Haynie

I once showed Pat Bradley my swing
and said, "What do I do next?"
Pat replied, "Wait till the pain dies down."
Bob Hope

The reason the pro tells you to keep your head
down is so you can't see him laughing.
Phyllis Diller

Try to find something joyful about each round
of golf, about each practice session.
Patty Sheehan

Golf is a natural course for women.
No sport that I can think of offers so much
satisfaction, so much enjoyment, and so many
benefits to women as golf does.
Sandra Haynie

When you think about it, of all the sports that
we all love to watch and become involved in, golf
is the only one that you can do as a child, play as
an adult, and then play with your grandchildren.
Judy Rankin

I expect to play golf until
I am 90 — even longer if
anybody figures out a way
to swing a club from
a rocking chair.

Babe Didrikson Zaharias

Let the ladies play through.

Golfing Adage

Sources

About the Author

Criswell Freeman is a Doctor of Clinical Psychology living in Nashville, Tennessee. He is the author of *When Life Throws You a Curveball, Hit It* and numerous books in the Wisdom Series published by WALNUT GROVE PRESS.

Dr. Freeman's Wisdom Books chronicle memorable quotations in an easy-to-read style. The series provides inspiring, thoughtful and humorous messages from entertainers, athletes, scientists, politicians, clerics, writers and renegades, with each title focusing on a particular region or area of special interest. Combining his passion for quotations with extensive training in psychology, Freeman revisits timeless themes such as perseverance, courage, love, forgiveness and faith.

Dr. Freeman is also the host of *Wisdom Made in America*, a nationally syndicated radio program.

The Wisdom Series
by Dr. Criswell Freeman

Regional Titles

Wisdom Made in America	ISBN 1-887655-07-7
The Book of Southern Wisdom	ISBN 0-9640955-3-X
The Wisdom of the Midwest	ISBN 1-887655-17-4
The Wisdom of the West	ISBN 1-887655-31-X
The Book of Texas Wisdom	ISBN 0-9640955-8-0
The Book of Florida Wisdom	ISBN 0-9640955-9-9
The Book of California Wisdom	ISBN 1-887655-14-X
The Book of New York Wisdom	ISBN 1-887655-16-6
The Book of New England Wisdom	ISBN 1-887655-15-8

Sports Titles

The Golfer's Book of Wisdom	ISBN 0-9640955-6-4
The Putter Principle	ISBN 1-887655-39-5
The Golfer's Guide to Life	ISBN 1-887655-38-7
The Wisdom of Women's Golf	ISBN 1-887655-82-4
The Book of Football Wisdom	ISBN 1-887655-18-2
The Wisdom of Southern Football	ISBN 0-9640955-7-2
The Book of Stock Car Wisdom	ISBN 1-887655-12-3
The Wisdom of Old-Time Baseball	ISBN 1-887655-08-5
The Book of Basketball Wisdom	ISBN 1-887655-32-8
The Fisherman's Guide to Life	ISBN 1-887655-30-1
The Tennis Lover's Guide to Life	ISBN 1-887655-36-0

Special People Titles

Mothers Are Forever	ISBN 1-887655-76-X
Fathers Are Forever	ISBN 1-887655-77-8
Friends Are Forever	ISBN 1-887655-78-6
The Teacher's Book of Wisdom	ISBN 1-887655-80-8
The Graduate's Book of Wisdom	ISBN 1-887655-81-6
The Guide to Better Birthdays	ISBN 1-887655-35-2
Get Well Soon…If Not Sooner	ISBN 1-887655-79-4
The Wisdom of the Heart	ISBN 1-887655-34-4

Special Interest Titles

The Book of Country Music Wisdom	ISBN 0-9640955-1-3
Old-Time Country Wisdom	ISBN 1-887655-26-3
The Wisdom of Old-Time Television	ISBN 1-887655-64-6
The Book of Cowboy Wisdom	ISBN 1-887655-41-7
The Gardener's Guide to Life	ISBN 1-887655-40-9
The Salesman's Book of Wisdom	ISBN 1-887655-83-2
Minutes from the Great Women's Coffee Club (by Angela Beasley)	ISBN 1-887655-33-6

Wisdom Books are available at fine stores everywhere.
For information about a retailer near you, call toll-free 1-888-WISE GIFT.